Sampson Low
2nd Print

for Natalie, Effie and Jess

© Sampson Low Ltd
First published in Great Britain in 2013
SLB0002
ISBN 978-0-9534712-3-2
This books is number 48 /100

Introduction

Life is a delicate balance. Drift in a perfect bliss of ignorance and you can find your personal Nirvana or find yourself lost. Structure our unpredictable lives and we harness our potential, achieve greatness or send ourselves to the edges of insanity.

So when I contacted our 1000+ artists with the book's theme, I felt more like a therapist and just a little bit unhinged myself. The task was to analyse their lives and to root out the personal systems that helps them function in life and work. I suspected that artists and authors were excellent exponents in the secret art of system making, with the flair and skill to explain them. What I hadn't expected was such a swift and varied response: within 6 hours of the call-to-arms we had to close submissions and the pages of the Patternotion book were all reserved.

We at Sampson Low Ltd are unusual in the way we select our artists and authors..... Everyone is welcome. We run a first-come first-served basis and have never rejected an entry. This has given the book a varied palette of ideas from artists, authors, children, train drivers, research directors, company bigwigs and unemployed geniuses from all over the world including England, Scotland, Wales, Denmark, Bosnia and Herzegovina, France, Germany, USA and for the first time The Democratic Republic of Congo.

The book is split into two sections. The first contains both prescriptive and open systems that may require some thought. In the second part I asked 9 artists to interpret systems from the previous section. With a mix of instinct and structure they have channelled their intellects, producing fascinating and unexpected results.

Read the book and you realise that a good system contains as few ingredients as possible and has a short shelf-life before being re-invented or adapted. In this book you'll find over 60 recipes to inspire and amuse you. In its best known form a life system is the New Year's Resolution, where the participant declares their intentions and like a social gladiator lives or dies under the gaze of the populace.

Patternotion is not a dramatic .... it is just a book. Read it though and the ideas inside could influence th

Alban Low 2013

Information on artists and their individual websites can be found at www.patternotion.blogspot.com
To buy books and other publications from Sampson Low Ltd then visit - www.sampsonlow.com

Patternotion

Part 1

Siobhan Tarr - Destination Unknown

This year, once a month, one of our family of 5 will plan and organize a day out to who knows where. You can't beat a good old mystery tour, there's a special thrill in not knowing where you're going or what's in store.

Lots of unknown fun and adventures to be had by all.

WALKING

Eskild Beck

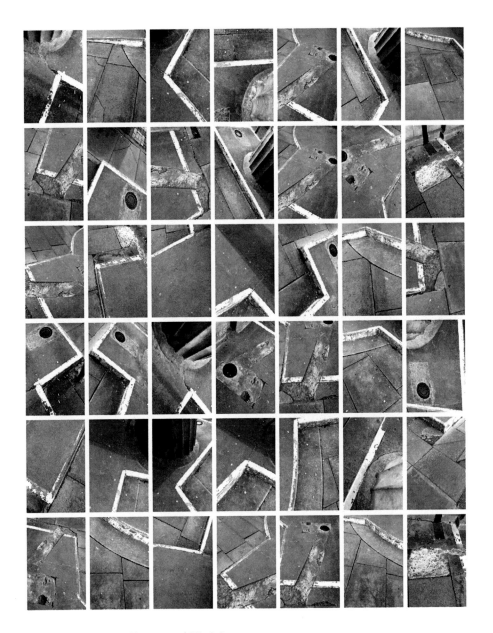

Mark Lomax - Walking and Waiting

Records the frustration and boredom of waiting for someone who is three quarters of an hour late for a meeting. The pattern created, with its zig zag rhythms and sense of movement, documents the erratic pacing and growing concern I was experiencing at the time. The images for this composite were taken using an ipod, this has since become my camera of choice.

THE RUSH HOUR

The Rush Hour is like a monstrous tidal wave
that surges into the day,
roaring through the city
with its powerful momentum.
It gobbles up the workforce and the schoolchildren
and propels them,
each to their own familiar destination.
Every worker and schoolchild
is transported, hurtling through the crowds
to their appointed desk.
The working day begins; the rush is over.
The streets are empty and quiet.

Now it is safe to venture out.
The mothers and babies, the unemployed,
the convalescents and the retired
gradually emerge.
We, who are retired, have no daily destination.
No-one is pulling our strings.
There are no rules.
We do not have those focused faces
or purposeful gait.
We no longer have a desk
and can wander in any direction
at our own pace –
but we have no map.

Yet half-shy, half-glances of recognition
reveal a silent, shared understanding
that we are all on the same path
and ultimately heading
in the same inevitable direction.

Sally Cockburn

Ella Penn - Two little words

I console myself with the justifications for failed attempts previous,
the wrong time, the wrong headspace. Resolved to begin again each year at the stroke
of midnight, ready and willing to step forth with a renewed sense of purpose.
I have vowed time and time again, repeating the same mantra, 'this is the year!
All too often falling far short of even the one-month hurdle.
But I see it now as clearly as I see these words; my pattern of failure was down to two
little words at a moment of weakness and they really aren't the answer.

Tim Cullingford - The Wrestler

I need to find a new artistic system.
I don't want to need to drink before every drawing. This is me, wrestling with myself in
the charity shop where I work. Inspired by the film

I may not be a religious man but...
"Dear God of second chances and
new beginnings... here I am again."

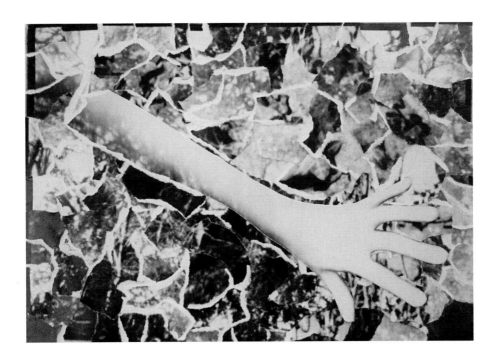

As artists we hoard old work, sometimes for years.
To me this is not a healthy state of affairs and as such my artwork
revolves around reusing my old work.
'The Spirit of Man' is based on an original darkroom print from a
pinhole photograph that was in my degree portfolio.
Hours of work went into producing the original print on expensive
heavyweight paper.
To rip it up and destroy it is something which was wonderfully
therapeutic (and anarchic) to do.
This new piece is better in this new reassembled state.
It is even more precious and meaningful now because it bridges
a whole timespan in my life rather than
one specific moment.

Melanie Ezra - The Spirit of Man

Sarah Beinart- Renaissance

After years of feeling creatively stifled, gradually petrifying in the dullest of jobs, stumbling along the same tracks and apparently not able to veer off the prescribed route, I have now finally worked up the courage to reinvent myself as a guitar-strumming, pencil-toting, yarn-bombing experimentalist living by the sea. Hopefully.

Wisdom

Strings strung
webs spun,
only to be met
by the wind.

Lines drawn
upon faces,
discolor light
and time.

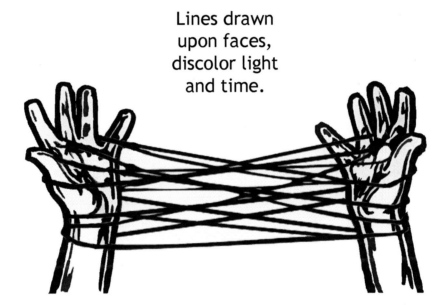

Tom Hosmer

When I was really quite young, I remember browsing through the local Woolworth's Five & Dime. There was a middle age couple dressed in working class clothes, who were standing silently staring into space not saying anything for some minutes, and then conversing and then silence again. I stood some distance away from them watching. They went on for a number of minutes in this manner. Even in this mime I could imagine the words exchanged and the thoughts which were held in silence.

After a while I moved on, but I realized that they were agonizing over a decision to make a purchase, and that the purchase would impact them in a very deep way financially. And, as I have walked through life I have seen this same scene play out in differing ways not only across this country but in different nations over the globe. Even in rich cities and countries, you can see the Invisibles if you just stand in one place long enough and watch.

Illustration by Alban Low

Sara Lerota

Title of story:
Every day is a new beginning

Title of artwork:
Dawn

Medium:
acrylics on canvas

Take a favourite milk jug, a teapot and a cup
Using pen and paper, start to sketch it up
Draw the patterns varied, sizes large & wee
Take a break, have a stretch, drink a cup of tea

Back to flowers and zig zags, yellow red & green
Not as colours really are but what the mind has seen
Add some black for drama, white to lift the tone
Tidy, neaten where I can & take the drawing home

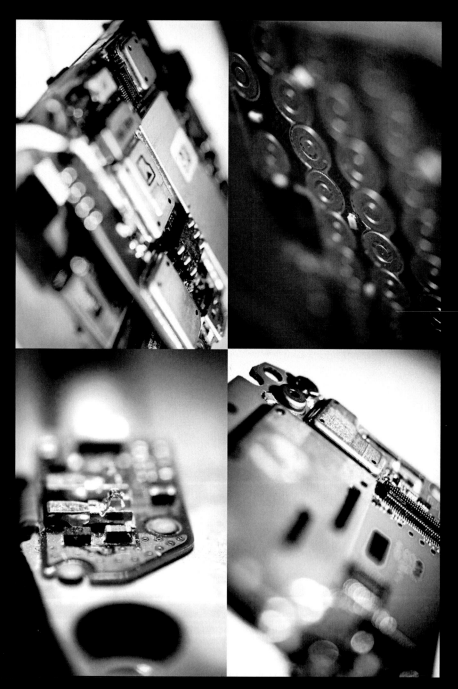

Darren Atkinson - Constantly Connected

We live in exponential times. Never before in history have human beings been so connected, yet dissonance pervades. The deconstruction of a Smartphone provided the inspiration for this architectural exploration of a constantly connected landscape.

I pay attention to the weather when I'm on deadline now.
Storm clouds gathering on the horizon tell me I need to hurry.
Rain usually means that the power will go out, taking the Internet connection with it.
It could be hours, or even days if I'm really unlucky, before it returns.
It wasn't like this in London.
But things are different in the Congo.
I have to type faster as the thunder gets closer, rushing to get the last bits done, doing a quick triage of what can stay and what can go.
I've learned that I have until the wind arrives to finish.
The wind always comes before the rain, blowing leaves and bits of litter and dust sideways and up, bending the palm trees and sending people scurrying for shelter.
When the first sheet of rain lashes the window by my desk I know that I need to file.
I may not get another chance for a while.
It wasn't like this in London.
But things are different here.

Thomas Yocum

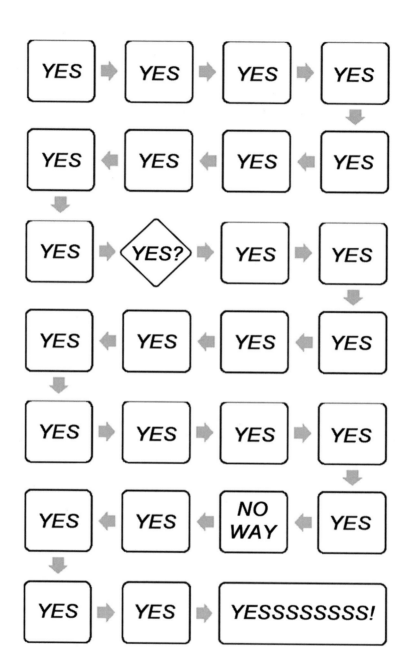

Jess and Alban Low
Wallpaper secrets

It's taken us many years to decorate Jess' bedroom
and remove it from the 'to-do' list. As we peeled away the old
wallpaper I found a date and a hand written note underneath.
A little research revealed this is a communication system used by
many in D.I.Y. Britain to record the act of wallpapering and also the story of their lives.
Unlike some, I discovered our message was brief and mysterious -
'1950.1967 Maybe this will be the last time....'.
Now Jess and I have painted the walls, the message is lost forever but not the sentiment.
We've continued the tradition by creating these sculptures from the detritus we
found under the floorboards and hidden in the nooks and crannies.

Laurette Carroll - Transformation
Transformation - moving from mind to paint with memory landscape.

Renata Szur - View Through My Bedroom Window - Day 19, 2012
The imprint of my palm on the glass. I wanted to know, how does it feellike being outside.

I have broken through old patterns and fears; quit nicotine, caffeine, microwave, meat, television and sneaking fares.
Been tapping into the unknown and just listening to the voice that speaks inside.
In the listening I am given all the guidance I need to do the right thing at the right time.   21

The collected philosophies of Jubilee Saffron-Beeton

These might not be for everyone. Salad cream, of course, has its place. But I have carefully considered the following maxims and they may save others the job of thinking all this through.

1. **Hairdressers.** Avoid. They are misguided and can be dangerous. Just ask my housemate Jo and her hairdresser friend Jenna, who attempted a surprise makeover of the Beeton barnet. Luckily, my ginger fro and I escaped through the toilet window before it was turned into an asymmetric side sweep with curly bits, straight bits and a strawberry tint. However, in the resulting tumult, Jenna embedded her scissors in Jo's foot and they both wound up in A&E.

2. **The Star and Pineapple**, St Paul's, Bristol. The place to be.

3. **Cider.** The only sensible choice of drink in the above. But don't let Dutty Del mix yours with blue WKD. This blend can cause lapses of memory where, for example, you might wake to discover that some miscreant has consumed your Fray Bentos pie-in-a-tin and, following a thorough investigation of your housemates, discover tell tale signs of gravy on your own chin.

4. **Fantasy gaming/second lives.** I was a firm opponent of this sort of leather-trench-coat-wearing, orc-collecting escapism. However, in alone one night I stumbled upon Sophie's boyfriend's laptop and found it can be quite diverting. Unfortunately for his avatar, Alandreas, my intense coffee consumption, technical ineptitude and attempt at virtual seduction proved almost terminal. His reaction to this news did indeed prove terminal for his relationship with Sophie. Approach with caution.

5. **Mayonnaise** – yes. Aioli – yes. Salad cream – no.

6. **Voting in elections**. It's very simple. You just have to look at the long view. I have observed that throughout all the red, blue, red, blue, things generally have improved and we've all become more rational and liberal. Consider the upward progression from the feudal system to universal suffrage and improved cider storage techniques. I'm not saying everything's perfect, but if we make sure they keep taking turns, we'll get there in the end.

7. **The Today Programme.** Use in moderation. Likewise Newsnight, which can be very bad for your sex life.

Catherine Steele

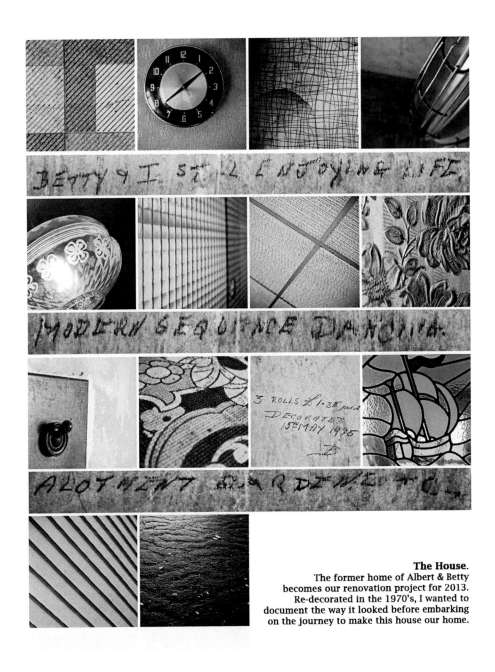

The House.
The former home of Albert & Betty becomes our renovation project for 2013. Re-decorated in the 1970's, I wanted to document the way it looked before embarking on the journey to make this house our home.

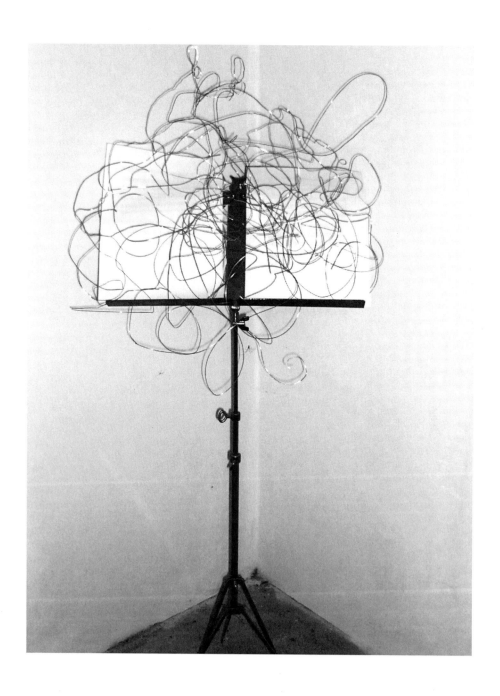

Wayne Sleeth - Listening to music for strings

Julia Colquitt Roach - Ridden
Started after overhearing a conversation between two women behind me, on a twenty minute bus journey

25

David W Ryan - Dawn Rider
Cycling to work on dark January mornings

Paul Jerram - Practice Philosophy

The mode of thinking I have adopted and extended from my everyday living into my Fine Art practice is the idea of recycling in its broadest sense. Being able to make greater use of the materials I have around me or that I am presented with each day, for example junk mail. This is something I would always feel very negatively about, but now I see a variety of possibilities and I find that I actually welcome it. My studio has become a mini recycling depot and it has allowed me to a gain a deeper resonance with recycling as a way of life. I allow the materials I have to hand guide what I am making and I consider my role as an artist as being simply an organiser.

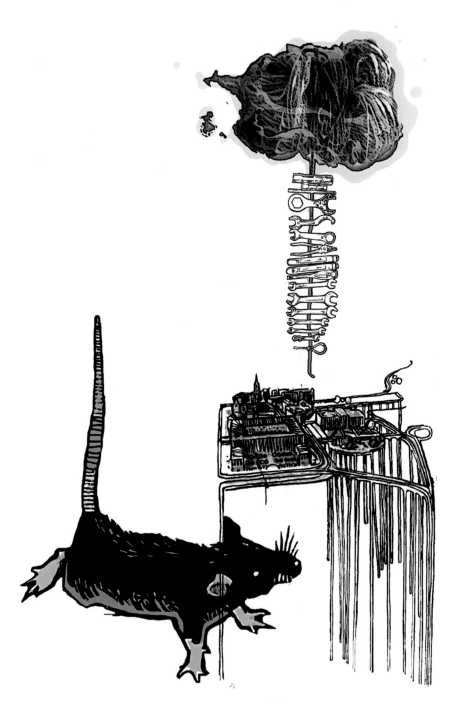

Alban Low - Foreground music
I listened to a whole album without distractions and this is what it made me think about.
The Ollie Howell Quintet - Sutures and Stitches

Stuart Simler - Sense of Space

This piece kicks starts a new theme of exploration for me and one which has also re-united me with some of my early inspirations of mark making and experimentations into the application of materials. The context for these new works are part of my forthcoming investigations into blind art and the way in which we perceive our surroundings with our senses and 'if' it is possible to communicate this through paint and media..........

Francesca Centioni - In-between

Peter S Smith - A Month of Sundays
between 29 and 31 drawings

31

Holly Daniels - Warnings & Ransoms

As an editorial artist, I know that the cartoons I produce won't change anyone's
political opinion; at best a cartoon enlightens and provokes debate,
at worst events have moved on by the time of publication and the cartoon
makes little sense at all. From my own perspective, these cartoons are my way of trying to
reclaim a little bit of control in a world in which democratic choice is limited and power is put
into the hands of the few who aren't necessarily concerned for the many.
In other words, drawing cartoons gives me the infantile ability to say: 'Yes, I know I can't do
anything about you and what you stand for, but look, don't you have a funny nose!'.

Alexandra Constantine - Inventory of idle creativeness
Artwork made from past doodles

33

Stella Tripp

Carry on with your artwork whatever else happens and remain positive.
If you can break through the negativity of a 'Do Not' attitude it will
become a motivating 'Keep Going'.

God has left us no script. He has vouchsafed us
no reasons for living. We are condemned to
create our own, ex nihilo.

We have to choose.

Lives of quiet plagiarism: believe what others believe;
say what others say; buy what others buy.
Smile vapidly; and then die.

Or lives we
choreograph
ourselves:
see with our
own eyes;
build our own
realities;
be both artist
and artwork.
Make our
own imprint in
the cosmic
wax.

Which way to go?   It's up to us.

Patten Smith - God's Script   35

the Starting Point

My social erotic photography is rooted in project ideas. Part of my inspiration comes from the sex industry and its many facets, the rest is intuitive. I believe my work is about enjoying the unspoken, praising the body and its social context. The creation process is one devoid of commercial pressures, and takes shape through a natural organic process. And like a fine wine laden in an oak barrel, my projects mature before seeing the light of day.

For the series entitled 'Call Me'

This series is an acknowledgement of the world's oldest trade, and focuses on one of its localised methods of promotion.

This collection started with the tart cards that can be found in central London public phone boxes. This is a whole level of communication between prostitutes and their potential clients that survives today, despite (or because of) mobile phones (and their memory storage), and the internet. The carded phone booths are located in both tourist and business areas.

After collecting numerous tart cards, I produced photo shoots with the models 'dressed' with these cards

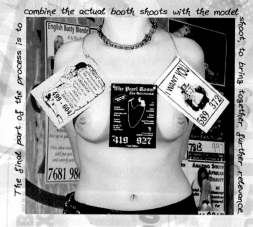

combine the actual booth shoots with the model shoot, to bring together further relevance.

The final part of the process is to

The card images used are not a true representation of the actual women on the end of the phone, but as far as the caller is concerned, the goods on offer are available.

Steve DT
www.sdtfoto.com

CRITgroup

Collaborative Project

CRITgroup was started in 2011 by graduates from MIRIAD (Manchester Institute for Research and Innovation in Art and Design) at Manchester Metropolitan University but is open to creative practitioners at any stage in their career. It aims to facilitate an informal opportunity for those working in a broad range of disciplines to meet, share and discuss their practical work as well as issues impacting on their practices, be those professional or otherwise.

At the inaugural meeting in November 2011 the possibility of a collaborative project was raised. After our first year of Creating, Reflecting, Investigating and Talking, we are now pleased to present initial stages in our first collaboration.

We are interested in investigating the perceived differences between 'art' and 'craft', as this has been a feature of our conversations in several meetings. How does the apparent need to 'label' oneself as a particular kind of practitioner (a 'photographer', a 'craft worker', etc.) affect individual practices and how do those descriptions of discipline relate to differing methods of producing work?

To get started, we are running three 'mini projects', which we will use in order to pin down and agree a clear research question that will then inform the next working stages of the project. The idea of these is that by introducing particular boundaries or criteria we will flush out key aspects of our respective practices which will better equip us in our collaborative investigations.

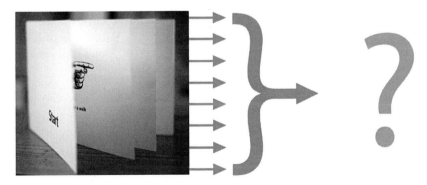

CRITgroup
Annabeth Orton, Kevin Linnane, Renate Wendel, Christine Wilcox-Baker, Irena Siwiak Atamewan, James Sharp, Shirley Hammond and David Hammond.

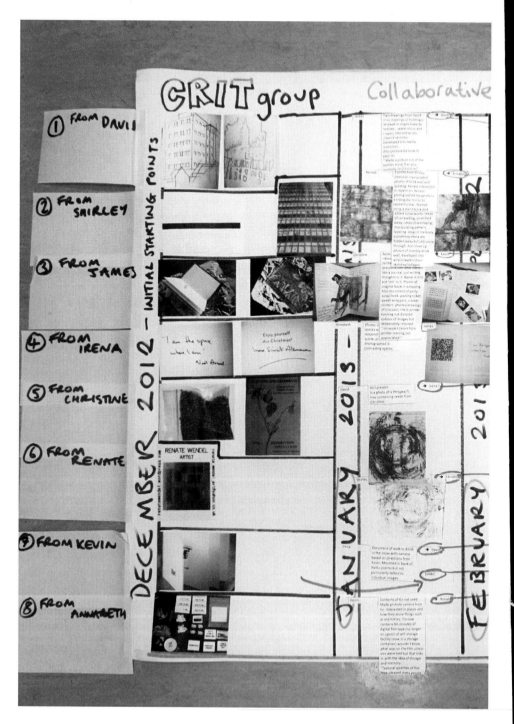

MARCH 2013 - RESPONSE 3

APRIL 2013 - RESPONSE 4

MAY 2013 - FINAL SHARING

CRITgroup

Details of proposed collaborative starting points as agreed at the November 2012 meeting:

Creative Whispers

Each collaborator produces 'a thing' (this maybe a physical object or just an idea recorded in a written/sketched fashion) which they feel somehow represents their practice. These are brought along to the next meeting (beginning December 19th), pooled and then picked out at random. The tasks is then to take that new outcome away, respond to it in some way (it may be to physically add to or develop an object, produce an outcome based on an idea, etc.) and bring it back the following month. These developed outcomes are then passed on to a new collaborator and the process will repeat until everyone has had some input on each starting point. We will then discuss and review the outcomes with a view to being in a better position to derive a clear 'question', though we will also undoubtedly have some interesting pieces in their own right.

Crafting by Committee

Each collaborator will produce a brief project proposal, situated within their current practice. The rest of the group will then act as a panel who will, upon hearing the proposal, specify particular criteria for how the project must progress. The practitioner must then follow these instructions precisely and return to the panel in a future meeting with the outcome. We can then use these pieces to reflect upon how decision making within different practices can impact upon outcomes but also be an intrinsic part of the creative process. Again, these will be research pieces, starting points for potential development and pieces of work in their own right.

Artists Anonymous

Proposed as a potential performance/audience participation piece at an event or opening in which we display work, this would again be part artwork, part research. Individuals in the group would be required to wear name tags which identify a creative discipline to which they ascribe themselves. In a parody of a 'self-help' session, they would be asked to introduce themselves to the group by specifying the particular practice which they feel they operate within and will then be 'interrogated' to justify or substantiate this claim. Though this will be facilitated by CRITgroup attendees, it's hoped to involve a wider range of individuals who might be somewhat unsuspecting and bring a whole new perspective to the conversation. This would probably be filmed and transcribed for further analysis.

Upon completion of these projects (as well as throughout), it is planned that collaborators will meet for a review session in which we will reflect upon the outcomes of each and discuss ways to move the project forward. This will include the formulation of a 'research question' which defines our area of investigation with more clarity.

If you would like more information about CRITgroup, please visit:
www.glittermouse.co.uk/critgroup.html
or contact us at CRITgroup c/o MadLab, 36-40 Edge Street, Manchester, M4 1HN

'About Time'
Sometimes I can't draw what I see... I can only draw how I feel.
My sketchbook studies document and express my thoughts and feelings.
I work intuitively layering patterns, maps, words and symbols.
I draw, scan, print... paint, tear, glue... then change it all on photoshop!

Carole Robinson

Shona Davies and Dave Monaghan
The Wheel of Misfortune offers glimpses of hospital environments as a reminder of mortality. The portals are stepped to echo a helix as the wheel rotates. After 5 seconds of movement the wheel comes to a halt and the viewer is confronted with a vision of their potential fate.

Rat run

Cut-through driving or Shortcut, is using secondary roads or residential side streets instead of the intended main roads in urban or suburban areas.

Vennel run

Cross town short cuts known to locals.

A vennel is a passageway between the gables of two buildings which can in effect be a minor street in Scotland. The word derives from French venelle, meaning 'little street', and is found in Scots texts from the fifteenth century onwards.

Keep your eyes on the road, your hands upon the wheel...
Roadhouse Blues

www.bluecranemedia.com/vennelrun

To immerse, initiate and allow.

Peacock Vow.

Daniel Leek

облаки дрейфуют следует как мой mi siga como mi sombra.
когда солнце этот тень. не облаки ¿No son nubes
деня прохождения лошады судбы? los caballos del destino?
начинается выхо- nubes se dejan llevar clouds drift
дить навсегда~ они cuando el sol de pasar as the sun of this day's
несут последний de este dia empieza passing begins to go
его света... всё marcharse para siempre away forever. They carry
как не возвра- llevan la última de su the last of its light. All
щает меня luz.. Todo lo que no vuelve that does not return
follows me like my shadow.
Are not clouds,
the horses of destiny?

David M Carroll - Clouds Drift

Following the publication of the fifth natural history book I have written and illustrated I have gone forward by turning back to visual art, working in ways largely set aside during my 23 year book epoch; and writing fragments in English and the foreign languages I pursue, at times interweaving visual and written elements.

Jess Goodyear - Home Survival Guide
How to get through the days and nights when your partner is elsewhere.

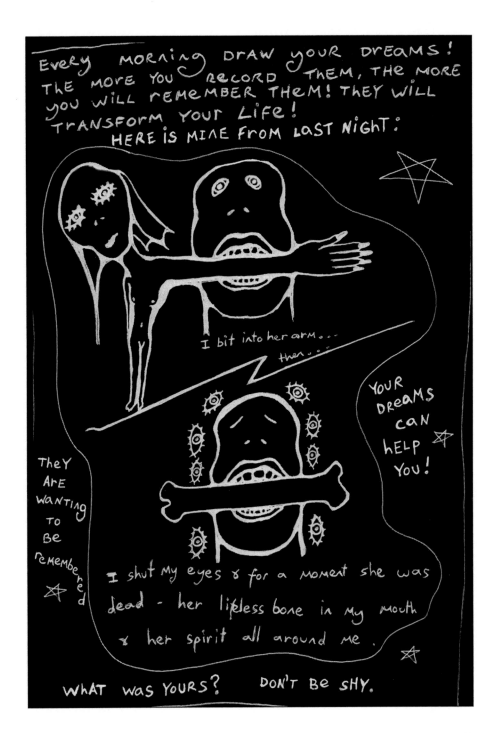

THE FUTURE IS NOT WHAT
IT USED TO BE
IT'S THE THINGS YOU
SAY YES TO WHICH
DEFINE YOUR
LIFE

Gwen Black - The Future

Theory

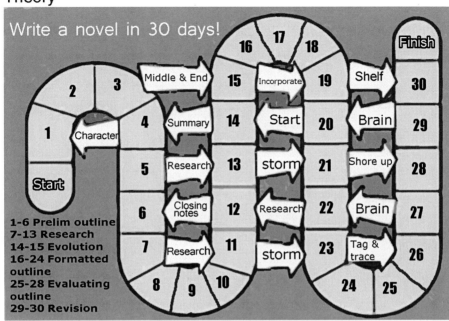

Practice

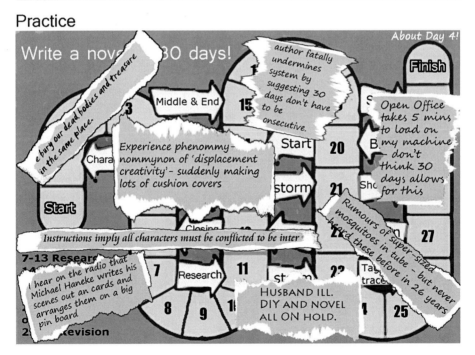

If you can observe your own experience with a minimum of interference, and don't try to control what you experience, if you simply allow things to happen and observe them, then you will be able to discover things about yourself that you did not know before. You can discover little pieces of the inner structures of your mind, the very things that make you who you are. In mindfulness, there is no attempt to make anything happen. There is nowhere to go. There is nothing to look for. Old habits don't go away. But we can create new habits. And we can learn to interrupt old habits when they come into conscious awareness, and change an old automatic reaction into a new conscious response.

Janet Soutar - In My Frantic Search For Knowledge
An expression of my desire to continue learning after doing the online course
"Modern and Contemporary American Poetry" last year which I thoroughly enjoyed.

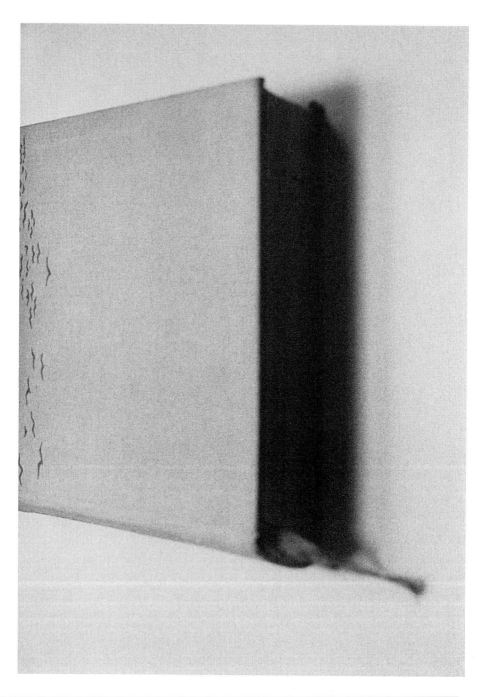

Monika Fischbein
The start of everything

Dawes Gray - How to Avoid the Temptation of Getting a Job (2013)

1) Select a range of items from a catalogue of your choice. 2) Calculate the amount of time that each item's price demands (living wage = £8.55 per hour). 3) Devote the correct amount of time to each item and create a new artwork that is in keeping with your current style. 4) Appear happy in your chosen vocation and relinquish any hopes of ever owning any of the items represented in your work.

Stumbled into the flat and smiled sweetly at my lovely Edith. I didn't immediately understand why she was giving me her "You are forgiven" look. I was just delighted to be gazing into those ketchup brown eyes again after so many hours away from her enchanting presence. Fumbled clumsily with the TV remote for six minutes or so before collapsing onto the sofa. Tucked energetically into my takeaway feast as the opening titles of the film Scanners appeared on the screen. Beautiful, adorable Edith rushed over with a large plate for my food and I suddenly realised that I was making quite a mess with my feeding frenzy. I kissed the nearest perfect cheek and whispered an incoherent message of love into her ear. Edith pulled a tissue from her pocket and methodically wiped away the greasy patches I had left on her skin. She gave me the Look again and I quickly turned my full attention to the screen. I knew from this films reputation that there would be unpleasantness aplenty including the occasional exploding head. I decided to chew on my burger during the non scary parts and save chips for the gory scenes. Chips have a simple purity which can be enjoyed even whilst witnessing the most gruesome spectacle. Only a DVD of The Exorcist has ever put me off my chips. A strange fellow I met at University was slapping me about the head and upper body with it at the time. In our final year he would attempt to blind me with a hotdog sausage but that's another story for another time. The point I'm trying to make here is that certain foods are an unsuitable accompaniment to the enjoyment of particular films, television programmes or indeed life in general. On the other hand, whatever the situation, the humble chip is always an appropriate and tasty treat. As I sprawled there enjoying great food, wonderful entertainment and the proximity of a very fine woman I remembered how my well meaning schoolteacher Miss Thomson had attempted to introduce my younger self to "good nutrition". It was an entirely new concept to me at the time. Often at home I had been encouraged to "eat up your scotch egg or you won't grow big and strong like Superman" but the thought of also cutting down on certain foods for the good of your health was a novelty. I was fascinated. Up until then I had not been a fussy eater. Absolutely anything put on my plate, save for the loathsome brussels sprout, would be devoured with pleasure. In future dining would become a much more complicated pastime. Important decisions would have to be made before even the tiniest morsel passed my lips. As luck would have it that evening's dinner consisted of burger and chips. I scoffed my burger greedily but made a point of leaving those delicious but deadly deep fried potato pieces on the side of my plate. My Mother was very patient with me. She explained that you should try your best at school, make sure that Miss Thomson is pleased with your work, but that you shouldn't try to apply any of that nonsense to real life. It was an important lesson to learn and I would later that day write in my diary that the chips were "yummy with no nutrition". That was before I met my Edith of course. Long before. It didn't really matter to me whether I lived a long and healthy life or not before I met Edith.

David Bushell - More Farted Against Than Farting

An excerpt from the bestselling autobiography that everybody's talking about

Anna Nilsen - Suspended in Time

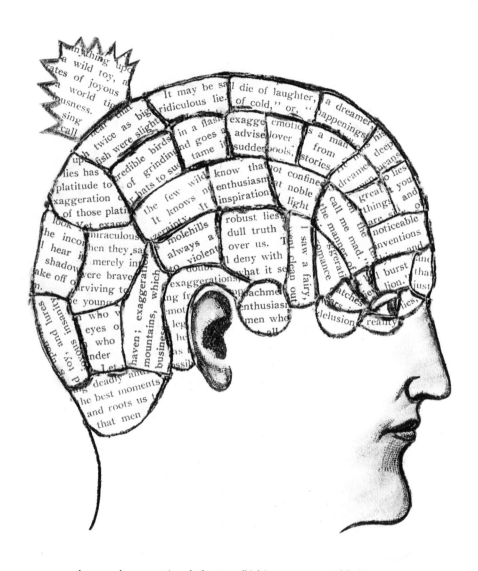

there must be exaggeration whether you call it lying or romance or delusion

Anne Guest - Anatomy of an exaggerated mind

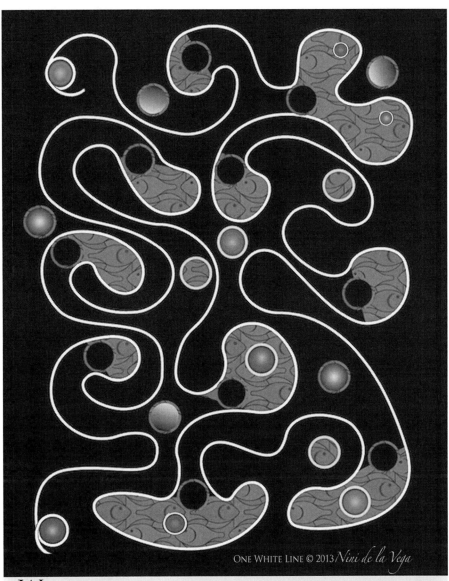

ONE WHITE LINE © 2013 *Nini de la Vega*

W here one beginning is not the end
and the end not closed nor disguised,
yet open to another side
neither narrow thin nor wide.
It is not tall nor pride exists
I follow with my eyes,
which guides the hand that drew one time,
one line so free, was just a pleasantry.

Hence, lost myself along the way, I've found the path again
it was existent, non resistant to the pull and push of pen.
A silence of the line, as a passenger I am
invoked a thought of happy with the map to buried treasure,
trials with fears and trails of tears are liquid smiles of pleasure
of what I do and try Oh well! Do tell me "nay or indeed"
the spirit of the mind I know "Not lost",
One line, one made, one time, one freed !

One Line © Nini de la Vega

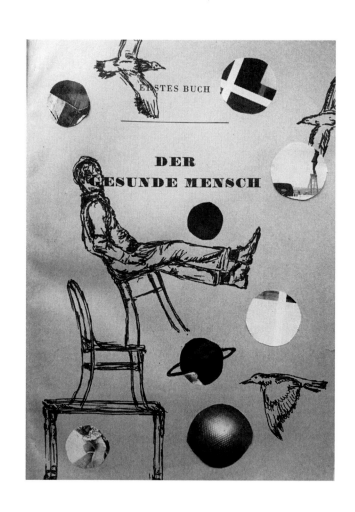

Ella Klenner - Keep the balance
After 2 weeks of a terrible flu the importance of a proper balance in Life
is more than ever a topic.

14th January, 2013 Conversation with Kath this morning .. motivations for our art work, K saying mine all political. All art has a political position, supports status quo if it doesn't challenge it.. her art subtly jolting perceptions in the world, and mine similar in forms and approach to materials but having feminist politics at its heart. ...she says Tai Chi approach is to deal with attack with curling away, and I dreamt last night of being attacked by a man, she asks what did you to, and I say I went for him with a chair and we both laugh cos lots of my work has been with chairs.. also I dreamt I was in the resistance in Eygpt pursued by army.. and then a man on a bus sexually harassed me and I challenged him outright only having 3 words of arabic . Shd I be trying to get into the mainstream art world more... I'd have to conform to the language and patterns of mainstream which is patriarchal and capitalist etc and really why shd I do this? Tho I do think feminist art shd be in every gallery if possible K's buddhist ...says everything she does is expressing her unique view of world and how to be in it. . I think I do the same as a feminist but nobody's perfect   Last night conversation about burlesque, is it feminist? .. seems to use the forms and stereotypes of patriarchy .. boobs and legs and masks and makeup, S says she feels freed by the events she's been to, and I say 'take me to the next one and I will try it'.. Judith Butler says we are all performing all the time... my life been more trying to get to what is me internally not the girl or woman I was forced to be by sexism and patriarchy .. starting in 1947 was a bit different from now.. I dont want to try on different personas.. but maybe I shd try more presenting myself as different people, wore a trilby to party last week and people said I looked good in it, and it was fun.. being a young women artist in 2013 very different.. same struggles with different faces.. now this book asks wht is my process this is my process wild knitting at the moment looking at corrective rape in S Africa and at women outsiders we don't mourn for yet those 200,000 women murdered in 16C for being different and resistant to the takeover of new male science of medicine (and quackery).. Those women midwives, herbalists, healers and maybe lesbians or hated patriarchy as much as I do and were forerunners of the suffragettes .. a group of young women invaded the ICA See Red poster event, with a poster which read 2013 STILL FIGHTING all we do shouldn't be a reaction I have made a new word now which means outside and beyond patriarchy isrupt isrupt isrupt

Caroline Halliday

Collaboration

I hate to make resolutions but I didn't want the year to start running away without having made any plans so I asked my artist friend, Cath, if we could collaborate and this is what she said,

Great idea
You give me a poem
I'll give you a painting
I'll give you the painting from the poem
You give me the poem from the painting
We can keep going
And see where it takes us?

So this year we will be having conversations between paintings and poems.

Watch this space
we'll be documenting Sonia's collaboration on the Patternotion website

Sonia Jarema

Patternotion

9 artists/authors were asked to interpret systems from Part 1.

Part 2

Peter S Smith - Figure in the Snow
Make a drawing using just one line (original system Page 57)

03:55am I went shopping and found SB working in Aldi he was wearing a green sweatshirt covering a yellow shirt and grey trousers he took me out back and told me he was going to show me the holistic suite he opened a heavy grey security door labelled staff only through this door was an executive luxury apartment with no windows he said so if you move in with us it is only £600 per month including bills but not including windows you'll have to pay more if you want windows in London I wanted to buy text books I walked for miles to try and find something suitable the sky was very grey and cold lots of traffic passed me but I don't remember seeing any people all the shops were closed I had the feeling that everyone had left because it was Christmas I met an elderly man beige trench-coat he told me that if I wanted books then there was a charity shop on the outskirts that may help me I thanked him and moved on the charity shop was along a stretch of shops in an old seventies style precinct it was the last shop on the right every shop was closed with whitewashed windows except for the charity shop which had a big sign in the window saying something here for everyone but not today because we're closed I wake up needing to pee with Jeff Wayne's War of the Worlds in my head.

07:30am I was jogging with AW we ran on concrete paths in a park we decided to race I got more aggressive in wanting to win so I pushed her she shoved me to the floor and ran off I picked myself up and ran home I realized I needed to change so I left this house to go to my real home where I found DL's family visiting they were supposed to bring Brother with them but he arrived a little while after in a red car which he said he'd hired I was suspicious because he hasn't got a license and his story didn't make sense because the car was an old red Montego DL said I didn't think he drove I said well he must've got his license and not told anyone upon questioning he admitted he'd borrowed it from a friend in Llanelli who in turn had borrowed it from someone else who lived out near Brecon DL climbed into a kitchen cupboard under the sink to try and impress me Brother was frying bacon and eggs he put the eggs in my sandwich followed by the bacon I took the bacon off and slowly and deliberately said no I do not have bacon I am veggie in response to this Brother deliberately put bacon again on my sandwich I said you do that again and I WILL FUCKING KILL YOU it was frozen slush underfoot and I'm now in a muddy car park on the side of a mountain somewhere near a supermarket I phone DL to ask if he is having the same weather the ground is crunchy and I'm enjoying making deliberate footprints in the brown muddy crust exit car park to find myself at a road junction H & K drive past me in a white Morris Marina the car turns right at the junction and into oncoming traffic H has to perform a three point turn in order to correct her mistake lots of angry drivers shout at her I wave to try to get H & K to notice me and say hello but they ignore me and continue on their journey I cross the road and am now driving a car with Unknown I am in the middle of a conversation about strange and funny school names I tell Unknown that my sisters went to a school called Chimmy Cheadle Chase I'm lying and no such school exists I keep insisting it's true even though I know deep down it's not my alarm wakes me I have No Doubt's Happy Now in my head.

Transformation

I can feel her smiling
through the radio -
the girl described by her friend
as welcoming all change.
While the bombs fell
she didn't cower,
just said what is death
but another adventure?
She glitters on the air
and I know my words
cannot bring her back to life
that I am not a doctor
that my nursing skills are close to zero
but maybe these words
could touch your arm
and turn your head
to see the light
the dark intensifies.
to see the light
the dark intensifies.

Sonia Jarema

Stuart Simler
Make a piece of art from intuition, just listening to the voice that speaks inside.
(original system Page 21)

Darren Atkinson - Every day is a new beginning
(original system Page 14)

In Tromso, locals celebrate the return of the sun, as each day gets longer and the ice flows morph and shift. At daybreak the changes are most profound as the ice murmurs and reshapes the landscape.

An Open-minded Walk
616 Gallery, Cambridge
February 7, 2013

i'll	left		left			one	right
just	right	left	right	left	left		left
pop		right		right	right	right	
in	left		left			left	right
for	right	left	right	left	it's		left
five		right		right	a	right	
minutes	left		left		big	left	right
	right	oh	right	left	gallery		
left		no		right		right	right
right	oooh		left		pause	left	left
	yuck	it's	right	left			
left		not		right	there's	right	time
right	left		i'm		more	left	i
	right	left	just	left	round		left
left		right	going	right	here	right	
right	left		to			left	right
	right	left	have	left	pause		left
hello		right	a	right	again	right	
anji	no		peek			left	bye
		hmmm	in	left	looks		anji
left	left		here	right	like	right	
right	right	pause		more		left	right
			left	left	of		left
that's	left	not	right	right	the	maybe	
nice	right	sure			same	not	that
		about	left	left	though		was
left	left	that	right	right		right	good
right	right	one			left	left	
			oh	left	right		right
left	left	left		right		right	left
right	right	right	left		left	left	
			right	left			pause
left	left	left		right	sudden	right	
right	right	right	left		pause	left	long
			right	left			pause
left	this	left		right	right	right	
right	one's	right	left		left	left	i
	a		right	wow			enjoyed
left	cy	left			that's	right	that
right	twombly	right	left	left	a	left	
	!		right	right	good		

20142015201620172018201920202021202220232024202520262027
20282029203020312032203320342035203620372038203920402041
20422043204420452046204620482049205020512052205320542055
20562057205820592060206120622063206420652066206720682069
20702071207220732074207520762077207820782080208120822083
20842085208620872088208920902091209220932094209520962097
20982099210021012102210321042105210621072108210921102111
21122113211421152116211721182119212021212122212321242125
21262127212821292130213121322133213421352136213721382139
21402141214221432144214521462147214821492150215121522153
21542155215621572158215921602161216221632164216521662167
21682169217021712172217321742175217621772178217921802181
21822183218421852186218721882189219021912192219321942195
21962197219821992200220122022203220422052206220722082209
22102211221222132214221522162217221822192220222122222223
22242225222622272228222922302231223222332234223522362237
22382239224022412242224322442245224622472248224922502251
22522253225422552256225722582259226022612262226322642265
22662267226822692270227122722273227422752276227722782279
22802281228222832284228522862287228822892290229122922293
22942295229622972298229923002301230223032304230523062307
23082309231023112312231323142315231623172318231923202321
23222323232423252326232723282329233023312332233323342335
23362337233823392340234123422343234423452345234723482349
23502351235223532354235523562357235823592360236123622363
23642365236623672368236923702371237223732374237523762377
23782379238023812382238323842385238623872388238923902391
23922393239423952396239723982399240024012402240324042405
24062407240824092410241124122413241424152416241724182419
24202421242224232424242524262427242824292430243134322433
24342435243624372438244394340244124422443244424452446447
24482449245024512452245324542455245624572458245924602461
24622463246424652466246724682469247024712472247324742475
24762477247824792480248124822483248424852486248724882489
24902491249224932494249524962497249824992500250125022503

Peter S Smith - The Future
(original system Page 48)

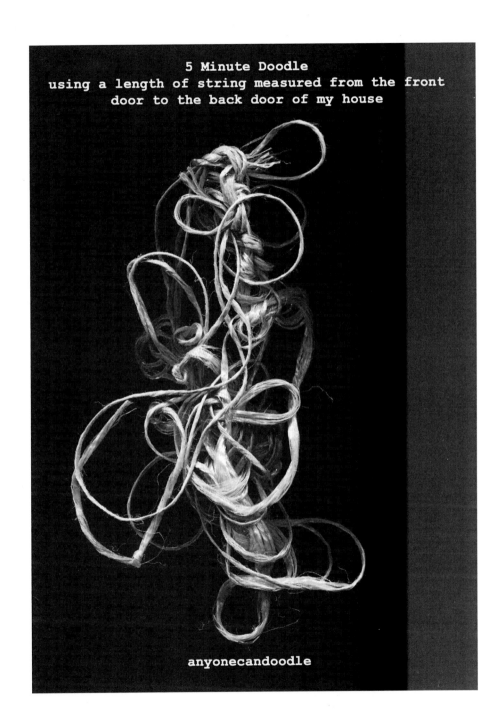

5 Minute Doodle
using a length of string measured from the front
door to the back door of my house

anyonecandoodle

Stephanie Wilkinson
Make an artwork from doodles. (original system Page 33)

"As sure as eggs is eggs my boy, you'll turn out just fine," said Symmetry to the newborn child Tessellation. It was the beginning of the tiled street pavement. In their two dimensional plane Shape and Symmetry lay beneath a contradicting sky of disorder; Tessellation set in fast, his work had already begun. He stamped and carried his parents across the exemplary grid and slowly they began to expand, like the bees' honeycomb that shelved itself as cells of harvest. Shape, Symmetry and Tessellation were united in conception, orchestrated by foreign design. Moved by biological shapes of inconsistent balance; cylindrical digits of wiggling, gripping, curling mass that sought always to manipulate. An idea of design from the designers; those who were more. Who create order from dysfunction and nurture Symmetry with intent. Calculators and constructors, measurers and librarians.

Shape and Symmetry are always and forever. Existing and to exist beyond the regions of any design. But for some minuscule moment in all of creation the concept of design means they are bounteous. They are beautiful and proportional and carry rhythm. Gifted with Tessellation the designers compose with subjective accuracy. To Shape and Symmetry the time they have in the hands of the designers is worth the eternity they spent without them.

Anatomy of an Exaggerated Mind

Ella Penn - Movements to an elaborate tune

Counting down the seconds in anticipation.

That troublesome place where the outcome is still to be decided, failure and success hang in the balance.

The decisive moment where fate begins to wave it's guiding hand.

In-between, the grey area, it belongs to both the beginning and the end, always on its way, but never a place of its own.

(original system Page 30)

422975

On the 9th March 2013 we organised a blue plaque walk to launch the Patternotion book. We did this in conjunction with Books For Free, a fanstastic organisation that rescues books and publications from pulping or landfill. We are indebted to Jacquelyn Guderley who rallied the literary troops in NW5 and made it a huge success. Find out more about this scheme at - www.healthyplanet.org/projects/books-for-free.aspx
We visited 20 blue English Heritage plaques of famous authors and poets as well as placing 50 of our own along the way.

Thank you to -
George, Sally, Sampson, Joshua and Jacob for supporting the book as a family and Sampson Low Ltd directors. Bill, Gina and Harriet Mudge, Rich and Chetna, Ollie Howell and his quintet, Harvey Wells, Eskild Beck, Jenn Ruppert, Lesley and Kelvin Christiane, Tom and Lizz Yocum, Ella Penn, our intern Philip Deed, Twickfolk and their regulars. Mark Coton (Pricewise), Peter S Smith and Mark Lomax who were the inspiration. And all the facebook people who have supported us and have their own
blue plaques reproduced here -

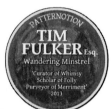

72